I. Introduction

In their capacity as consumers, many economists have no doubt wondered about the motivation behind the complex pricing strategies employed by supermarkets. Perhaps the most perplexing aspect of retail behavior is that the majority of supermarkets choose to offer a relatively small set of items (among the more than 35,000 items they typically carry) at a low "sale" price each week, and change that set virtually every week. Despite the high administrative costs of changing retail prices (Levy, et al., 1997), retailers clearly find it profit maximizing to put different items on sale each week. Recent empirical work documents this pattern. Hosken and Reiffen (2004a) and Aguirregabiria (1999) show that most goods can be characterized as having a regular price, and most deviations from that price are downward and temporary.[2] These infrequent temporary downward price movements are empirically significant, as they represent between 25 and 50% of the observed variation in retail prices (Hosken and Reiffen, 2004a). Hence, understanding why sales occur is an important element to understanding retail price variation.

Two classes of models have been developed to explain why retailers vary retail prices, independent of changes in wholesale prices. Both examine the pricing behavior of single product retailers, and show how consumer heterogeneity can lead to retail price variation over time. Varian (1980) is the seminal contribution of the first type of model. In Varian, consumers are heterogeneous in their willingness to search for low prices; some buy only at the first retailer they encounter, others compare prices and buy from the retailer offering the lowest price. Consequently, each retailer faces a tradeoff between charging a high price and selling only to consumers who do not search, versus charging a low price and potentially also selling to consumers who do search. Varian shows that the only symmetric equilibrium features mixed strategies, where all retailers choose their price from a continuous distribution with no mass points, which implies that each retailer changes his price each period. Hong et al. (2002) examine a variant of Varian's model where consumers can purchase for current as well as future consumption (inventory). Like Varian,

---

[2] This concept of a sale contrasts with other kinds of systematic price reductions that have been documented. One such pattern is that prices for goods with a "fashion" element often systematically decline over a fashion season (see, e.g., Pashigian (1988), Pashigian and Bowen (1991), Warner and Barsky (1995)), as retailers learn which styles are popular with consumers. We view this type of sale as a fundamentally different phenomenon than that examined here.

they find that the only symmetric equilibria feature mixed strategies in prices. Unlike Varian, they show that for certain levels of inventory there is a mass-point at the upper support of the pricing distribution.

The second type of model views sales as a means of price discrimination, see, e.g., Conlisk et al. (1984), Sobel (1984), and Pesendorfer (2002). The basic intuition of this modeling approach is that consumers differ in their reservation values and in their willingness to wait (which is analytically similar to differences in inventory costs). Low-value consumers are more willing to wait for price reductions because the cost of waiting is higher for the high-value consumers. Hence, only low-value consumers wait for the periodic price reductions. As a result, periodic price reductions allow a retailer to charge a low price to all low-value customers, while most high-value customers purchase at a higher price.[3] Similar to Hong, et al., this model predicts that prices will normally be at a high level with periodic discounts.

Both literatures provide useful insights into the forces generating retail sales. Recent empirical work, however, suggests that these models fail to explain important aspects of retail sale behavior. Specifically, five regularities about supermarket pricing drawn from the recent empirical literature are particularly relevant in modeling retail pricing dynamics. First, there is a large mode in the pricing distribution for all types of goods, in particular, both goods that can easily be stored, e.g., cola, and those that are highly perishable, e.g., bananas (Aguirregabiria (1999) and Hosken and Reiffen (2004a)). That is, most products have "regular" price. Second, most deviations from a product's modal price are price reductions (Dutta et al. (2002) and Hosken and Reiffen (2004b)). Third, most price reductions are temporary (Pesendorfer (2002), Hosken and Reiffen (2004a)). Fourth, short-lived reductions in retail prices often represent a decrease in retail margins rather than wholesale prices or manufacturing costs; that is, sales are often the result of retailer rather than manufacturer behavior (MacDonald (2000), Levy et al. (2001), Dutta et al. (2002), and Chevalier et al. (2003)). Fifth, some consumers respond to sales by purchasing more than they will consume

---

[3]   Lal and Matutes (1989) offer a similar explanation for why competing multiproduct retailers using different (static) pricing strategies for their array of goods. Because each retailer has a low price on a different good, retailers sell some items at high prices to high transportation-cost/high reservation-value consumers, while low transportation-cost consumers buy at more than one store each period in order to get low prices on all goods.

in the current period; that is, a subset of consumers respond to low prices by purchasing for household inventory (Pesendorfer (2002) and Hendel and Nevo (forthcoming)).

Comparing these recent empirical findings to the theoretical literature yields some inconsistencies between the theory and the evidence. Varian's model predicts an absence of mass points in the price distribution. The evidence, however, suggests that the price distributions of *all* types of products are characterized by relatively large point masses at the mode of the distribution, with short-lived discounts below this everyday price. The price discrimination models and Hong et al. generate pricing distributions consistent with these features of the data, and are consistent with recent evidence suggesting that consumers store the goods they buy at low prices for consumption in later periods. However, the price discrimination models only seem applicable for products that can be stored for later consumption. Goods that are both highly perishable and typically consumed each "period" (where period corresponds to the length of time between shopping trips), also have significant mass points in their pricing distributions.[4]

To explain price variation more generally, we draw on some insights developed in the literature on multiproduct retailers. What differentiates multiproduct retailers from single product retailers is that consumers can save transactions costs by buying a bundle of goods from the same retailer, rather than assembling that same bundle from numerous retailers. This implies that a multiproduct retailer is fundamentally different from a set of individual one-product firms who collectively carry the same group of products. For example, as Lal and Matutes (1994) show, consumers' preference for purchasing bundles of products implies that for some range of prices, a retailer's offer of a discount on any good in a bundle will have a similar effect on a retailer's likelihood of attracting a given consumer (who purchases all goods in the bundle at that retailer).

In this paper we determine equilibrium pricing behavior in a dynamic model in which competing retailers each sell two goods, a storable good that can be inventoried by consumers, and a perishable good that cannot. This model predicts that the prices of both goods will change

---

[4]   From a modeling standpoint, a good that is physically perishable, but for which consumers can "time" their consumption (fresh lobster, theater tickets) would be economically similar to a storable good. However, as Aguirregabiria (1999) and Hosken and Reiffen (2004a) show, mass points also appear in the pricing distributions of perishable goods that are typically purchased and consumed each period, e.g., milk, bread, bananas.

periodically, even though price discrimination through intertemporal price changes is only feasible for the storable. The model's pricing prediction are consistent with recent empirical findings: storable and perishable prices have high everyday (modal) prices with periodic discounts. In addition, we show that in equilibrium, price movements will be different for perishable and storable goods; storable pricing will feature long periods of stable prices, followed by significant but short-lived price reductions, whereas perishable prices will move more frequently, but by smaller amounts.

While our model and Varian's have different predictions about the shape of retail price distributions, the underlying intuition in both models is that retailers have sales in order to attract those consumers who choose between retailers on the basis of price. Both models find that, in equilibrium, retailers offer surplus to consumers every period, with the specific level of surplus drawn from an atomless, continuous distribution. Because Varian's retailers sell only one good, its price (and, equivalently, the surplus consumers obtain from each retailer) is drawn from an atomless distribution. By generalizing Varian's model to allow retailers to sell multiple products, we show that while surplus continues to be drawn from an atomless distribution, each product will have a mass point in its price distribution. The reason is that each product is an instrument for offering surplus, and it will generally be profitable to only use one instrument at any point in time. Hence, if the profitability of using one good as an instrument changes over time (e.g., as in the intertemporal price discrimination models), that can lead to changes in the relative profitability of using each good's price as an instrument for offering surplus. Thus, by incorporating the multiproduct nature of retailers' offerings into the model, we explain a richer set of observed retailer behavior.

II. A Model of Sales and Multiproduct Retailers

In this section we develop a model of competition among $N > 1$ multiproduct retailers. Each retailer sells the same two products to a unit mass of consumers. These products have different storage characteristics. The first good is *storable*, which means that consumers can purchase the good for current and later consumption. The second good is *perishable* and must be consumed during the period in which it is purchased.[5] We incorporate the multiproduct nature of the retailers by assuming that consumers can visit no more than one store each period. This implies that if consumers purchase both goods in a period they must purchase both from the same retailer.[6]

Our assumptions about consumer behavior are fairly standard.[7] We assume that all consumers consume at most one unit of each good in each period. Each consumer has measure zero and views prices as exogenous to his or her purchasing decisions. We also assume that a consumer's reservation value for each good is independent of the quantity consumed (and therefore the price) of the other good. Consumers are heterogeneous with respect to their costs of comparing prices across retailers, their valuations of the storable good, and their costs of storing the storable good (as in Sobel and Pesendorfer). Specifically, we assume there are two kinds of consumers; those who are store-loyal, and do not compare prices across stores (i.e., they have high search costs) and those who are shoppers, and evaluate stores on the basis of price. Store-loyals represent a portion γ ($<$ 1) of customers, and $1/N$ of them are loyal to each retailer, while the remaining $1-\gamma$ customers are shoppers. Store-loyals have higher reservation values and storage costs for the storable product than do shoppers; store-loyals have reservation values of s_H for the storable, which is higher than shoppers' reservation values (s_L). Finally, with respect to storage costs, we assume that store-loyals have no capacity to store the storable good (i.e., in effect, infinite storage costs), while shoppers all have capacity to store M units of it. This implies that while shoppers *consume* no more than one unit of each good in each period, they can *purchase* multiple units of the storable in a period.

We assume that consumers are less heterogeneous with respect to their reservation values

---

[5]   The distinction between storable and perishable goods can be thought of in terms of storage costs; perishable goods are those with high storage costs. From this perspective, the dichotomous distinction in the text simplifies the analytics, while maintaining the economic substance of differing storage costs. From a practical standpoint, goods will in actually vary from highly perishable (very costly to store), like raspberries or bread to moderately perishable, like hot dogs or yogurt, to highly storable, like paper towels or canned fruit.

[6]   This is a stronger form of the assumption in Lal and Matutes that every consumer prefers to make all of his or her purchases from the same retailer, reflecting a transaction cost of visiting each retailer.

[7]   We discuss the empirical validity of several of our assumptions in Section III.

for perishable goods than for storables. Specifically, we assume that all consumers have a common reservation value of β for the perishable (which is identical to the assumption in Varian). To reduce notational complexity, we interpret s_L, s_H and β as the differences between consumers' reservation values and the constant marginal cost of selling the good, so that we normalize retailers' costs to zero.

Given these assumptions, we derive a Markov perfect equilibrium in which the relevant state variable is consumer inventory. Similar to the equilibrium in Hong et al., firms condition on consumer inventories only, and the information available to consumers when making their purchasing decisions consists of all consumers' inventory holdings of the storable good and current prices. In each period, retailers choose a single price for each of the two goods (i.e., they cannot charge different prices to loyals and shoppers in any period), and those prices are observable to consumers prior to deciding which retailer to visit.

We begin by describing consumer purchasing behavior for the two types of consumers in our model: shoppers and loyals. A loyal consumer's optimal behavior is to visit her preferred retailer and purchase one of any good whose price is less than or equal to her reservation price. The shopper's decision making is more complicated. A shopper evaluates the prices of potential bundles they may purchase, and considers both current and expected future prices of the storable price in evaluating which retailer to visit in a period. Because the shopper is, in effect, evaluating retailers on the consumer surplus they offer, we introduce a variable that measures the consumer surplus associated with shopping at retail j at time t, $\Psi_{j,t}$. Given consumer decision making, it is possible to describe retailer behavior. Retailers compete on the basis of the consumer surplus they offer consumers (where the prices of the two goods are instruments to manipulate the level of consumer surplus they offer). We show (analogously to Varian) that retailers play a mixed strategy in the consumer surplus they offer consumers. We also show that the expected profits a retailer earns in any period are independent of consumer inventory holdings. We then prove that a retailer will never offer both the perishable and the storable on sale in the same period. To explicitly solve for an equilibrium, we make additional assumptions that guarantee retailers will only find it profitable to offer a sale on the storable in a period if all shoppers' inventories are zero. This implies that when shoppers observe a sale on the storable, they find it utility maximizing to purchase as much

6

of the storable as possible; that is, they purchase enough units of the storable such that their inventory holdings are M. Finally we solve for the equilibrium price distributions of the storable and perishable good. In contrast to previous models of sales, our model predicts (consistent with recent empirical evidence) that both perishable and storable goods will have mass points in their pricing distributions.

A. Consumers' Purchasing Behavior

The assumptions made above about consumers' reservation values, search costs and storage costs imply that store-loyals and shoppers react differently to a given set of prices. Let $P_{P,t}^j$ be retailer j's price for the perishable at time t, and $P_{S,t}^j$ be retailer j's the price for the storable at time t. Recalling that the reservation price for each good is independent of the price of the other good, a store-loyal customer will receive surplus of $\max\{(\beta - P_{P,t}^j), 0\}$ from buying the perishable at retailer j, and $\max\{(s_H - P_{S,t}^j), 0\}$ from buying the storable at retailer j. It follows that a store-loyal will visit her preferred retailer and purchase one unit of the perishable if $P_{P,t}^j \leq \beta$, and one unit of the storable good if $P_{S,t}^j \leq s_H$ and one unit of each if both inequalities hold.

The assumption that consumers can visit no more than one store per period implies that if a shopper purchases both goods in any period, then she buys both from the same retailer. That is, in each period each shopper must determine which retailer to visit and how much to purchase of each good. A shopper's welfare-maximizing choice of retailer is the one that offers the greatest consumer surplus, summed across the two goods. For this reason, the prices of both goods may be relevant to a shopper's purchasing decision, even though his or her demand for each good is independent of the other good's price. Further, because shoppers can inventory the storable good, the choice of retailer that maximizes a shopper's welfare depends on the inventory the shopper had entering period t and future storable prices.

Specifically, let $\Psi_{j,t}$ be the consumer surplus consumer k (who is a shopper) gets from choosing retailer j in period t.[8] A shopper's optimal retailer will be the one offering the highest $\Psi_{j,t}$. The surplus generated from choosing retailer j at time t will derive from consumption in period t and/or future periods. Given a shopper's purchasing decisions and inventory, her consumption choices follow directly. Since the perishable must be consumed during the period in which it was purchased, the purchasing decision for the perishable in period t determines its consumption in period t. In contrast, a shopper will choose to consume one unit of the storable if she has one or more units of inventory entering period t (i.e., $I_{t-1} \geq 1$) and/or if she purchases one or more units at time t. For example, if a shopper entered period t with $I_{t-1} = 0$ and purchased m (> 1) units at time t, she can consume one unit in period t, and one unit for each of the next $m - 1$ periods.[9] Conditional on visiting retailer j, a shopper will purchase one unit of the perishable if $P_{P,t}^j \leq \beta$. When $P_{P,t}^j \leq \beta$ and $s_L \leq P_{S,t}^j$, $\Psi_{j,t}$ is simply equal to $\beta - P_{P,t}^j$. That is, since the perishable

cannot be stored for future consumption, shopper k will buy exactly one unit of the perishable, and no units of the storable at those prices.

When $s_L > P_{S,t}^j$, one cannot, in general, write $\Psi_{j,t}$ as a closed form. This is because shopper k's surplus from buying the storable depends on shopper k's inventory of the storable, as well as expected future prices, which in turn depend on the inventory holdings of all shoppers. We assume that I_0 is the same for all shoppers, which in turn implies that for any given set of prices, $\Psi_{j,t}$ is likewise identical for all shoppers in period 1. One case in which $\Psi_{j,t}$ can be expressed as a closed-form, even when $s_L > P_{S,t}^j$, is where shopper k enters period t with inventory of I_{t-1} and believes that there will not be another sale on the storable at any retailer for $M + 1 - I_{t-1}$ periods (where M is the exogenous storage capacity of shoppers). In that case, if shopper k visits retailer j who has set $P_{S,t}^j \leq \delta^M s_L$ (where δ is the shopper's per-period discount factor), it will be optimal for her to

---

8 Formally, $\Psi_{j,t}$ is the difference between the surplus associated with consumer k's having the opportunity to buy at retailer j's prices in period t, and the surplus from not making any purchases in period t, for any given set of expected future prices. See Appendix B for details.

9 Note that, in contrast to M, which is the storage capacity of shoppers, m is an endogenous decision of shoppers.

purchase $M + 1 - I_{t-1}$ units of the storable, because if she buys fewer units, she will stock out of the storable before the next sale. Under those conditions, the closed-form expression for $\Psi_{j,t}$ is

$$\max\{0, \sum_{\tau=I_{t-1}}^{M} [\delta^{\tau} s_L - P_{S,t}^j]\} + \max\{0, \beta - P_{P,t}^j\} \qquad \text{for all } I_{t-1} < M.$$

A particularly tractable case is where all shoppers believes that a sale on the storable can only occur if $I_{t-1} = 0$ for virtually all shoppers (that is, all shoppers except perhaps for a set of shoppers with measure zero). We let $\mathbf{I_{t-1}}$ (in bold) be the vector of all consumers' inventories entering period t, so that the condition can be written as $\mathbf{I_{t-1}} = 0$. In that case, if shopper k has $I_{t-1} = 0$ and visits retailer j who has set $P_{S,t}^j \leq \delta^M s_L$ it will be optimal for her to purchase M+1 units of

the storable if she believes all retailers will set $P_{S,t}^j = s_H$ for the next M periods.[10] In Propositions 4

and 5 below, we show that for certain parameter values (see conditions 1 - 4) there is an equilibrium in which these beliefs by shoppers (i.e., a sale on the storable only occurs when $\mathbf{I_{t-1}} = 0$) are validated.

B. *Retailers' Behavior and its Implications for Consumer Surplus*

This subsection derives several properties of the symmetric equilibrium in the retail market. Principal among these are the finding that firms play a mixed strategy in terms of the $\Psi_{j,t}$ they offer

each period, and that they offer positive surplus each period. We also show that one product will be on sale each period.

Retailer j chooses $P_{S,t}^j$ and $P_{P,t}^j$ to maximize the present value of profits. In setting price,

each retailer considers the tradeoff between the profits he can earn by charging high prices and only

---

[10]   The assumptions in conditions (1) - (4) lead to an equilibrium in which shoppers have a simple purchasing rule. This allows us to obtain closed-form solutions for prices. However, the key condition for most of our results is that an equilibrium exists in which aggregate purchases by shoppers are increasing in the amount of time since the most recent sale on the storable. That condition is shown to characterize consumer behavior in a model with exogenous price shocks, but in which $\mathbf{I_{t-1}} = 0$ is not a necessary condition for a storable sale by Hendel and Nevo.

selling products to store-loyals versus charging low prices and potentially selling to shoppers as well. Profits from loyals are maximized at $P_{S,t}^j = s_H$ and $P_{P,t}^j = \beta$ (and, consequently, retailers will never charge more than s_H and β). As described above, a shopper's choice of retailer depends on the Ψ offered by the competing retailers, and the $\Psi_{j,t}$ are, in turn, a function of prices.[11] If retailer j sets $P_{S,t}^j = s_H$ and $P_{P,t}^j = \beta$, shoppers will get zero surplus ($\Psi_{j,t} = 0$), and the retailer's profits will be equal to $\dfrac{\gamma(s_H + \beta)}{N} + \dfrac{(1-\gamma)\beta}{N} \Pr(\Psi_{it} = 0 \text{ for all i})$. When all of j's rivals also set their $P_{S,t}^j > s_L$, no shopper buys the storable, and hence all shopper's inventories will be reduced by one unit (if they have positive inventory). Alternatively, the retailer can offer a "sale" on either the perishable (by setting $P_{P,t}^j < \beta$), the storable (by setting $P_{S,t}^j < s_H$), or both. If a retailer chooses to have a sale, he will forego some profits that could be earned from the loyal customers (in addition to potentially increasing shoppers' inventory if the sale is on the storable). However, if the retailer offers the highest Ψ in period t, he will earn additional profits by selling to shoppers.

We are interested in deriving a symmetric Markov-perfect equilibrium in which retailers optimally choose prices each period, and likewise consumers make optimal purchasing decisions. Because of the relationship between prices and $\Psi_{j,t}$, we can construct the equilibrium in terms of Ψ, with the understanding that whatever Ψ is chosen will be offered by choosing the profit-maximizing prices associated with that Ψ. Proposition 1 generalizes Varian's (1980) result regarding the equilibrium distribution of prices for single-product retailers. Varian shows that the symmetric equilibrium in that case features a mixed strategy, whereby all retailers draw their prices from a continuous, atomless distribution.

Proposition 1: If all shoppers begin period 1 with a common inventory of the storable, then the

---

symmetric equilibrium features all retailers playing a mixed strategy with respect to Ψ. The distribution of Ψ, $G(\Psi|\mathbf{I}_{t-1})$

    A. Has no mass point.

    B. Has a lower support of zero

Proof: See Appendix A.

Proposition 1 implies that if there is a symmetric equilibrium, at least one product will be on sale in every period in that equilibrium. The intuition is very much the same as in Varian; if all other retailers were not having a sale (i.e., setting $P_{S,t}^{j} = s_H, P_{P,t}^{j} = \beta$ so that $\Psi_{j,t} = 0$), any individual retailer could profitably offer $\Psi_{j,t} > 0$ (e.g., by setting $P_{P,t}^{j}$ slightly less than β), and make sales to all shoppers. As in Varian, in the symmetric equilibrium, retailers do not offer any specific $\Psi_{j,t}$ with a positive probability; instead in every period Ψ is drawn from a common atomless distribution function. The key departure from Varian is that Proposition 1 implies that in equilibrium either good's price can be equal to the consumers' reservation value for that good, as long as the other price is not.

Even though there cannot be a mass point at $\Psi_{j,t} = 0$, the lower bound on the support is zero, so that setting $P_{S,t}^{j} = s_H$ and $P_{P,t}^{j} = \beta$ yields a Ψ in the support of $G(\Psi|\mathbf{I}_{t-1})$, and yields a profit of $\gamma(s_H + \beta)/N$. This in turn implies that expected profits at any set of prices that retailers choose to offer are equal to $\gamma(s_H + \beta)/N$, and therefore independent of $\mathbf{I}_{t-1}$.

Proposition 2:

A. Expected retailer profits from any $P_{S,t}^{j}$, $P_{P,t}^{j}$ in the equilibrium set of prices (i.e., every Ψ in the support of $G(\Psi|\mathbf{I}_{t-1})$) are $\gamma(s_H + \beta)/N$, and independent of $\mathbf{I}_{t-1}$.

B. $G(\Psi)$ represents a symmetric equilibrium.

Proof: See Appendix A.

Thus, $G(\Psi)$ constitutes an equilibrium. In every period, expected retailer profits are equal to $\gamma(\beta + s_H)/N$, independent of shoppers' inventory holdings of the storable good. The logic is that retailers are essentially homogeneous Bertrand competitors in selling to shoppers, and hence, in equilibrium, do not earn profits from selling to shoppers. Although it would be profitable, in expectation, to price discriminate by occasionally lowering the price of the storable *if* other retailers kept their storable price at s_H, competition between retailers to attract shoppers when inventories are low results in a dissipation of the gains to a firm from price discriminating (as in Sobel).

Propositions 1 and 2 relate to the equilibrium property of the symmetric distribution of Ψ. We now turn to the relationship between Ψ and prices.

Since all retailers have at least one product on sale every period, we next consider the profitability of alternative types of sales. There are three kinds of sales; a sale on the perishable only, a sale on the storable only, and a sale on both goods. Retailer j's profits from having a sale on the perishable only (i.e., $P_{P,t}^j < \beta, P_{S,t}^j = s_H$) are the profits from the store-loyals, plus the expected profits from the shoppers, or:

$$\frac{\gamma(s_H + P_{P,t}^j)}{N} + (1-\gamma)P_{P,t}^j * Pr(\Psi_{j,t})$$

where $Pr(\Psi_{j,t})$ is the probability that retailer j is offering more surplus than all of the other N–1 firms at time t.

The other two possibilities are to have a sale on the storable only, or to have a sale on both goods. In either case, the firm's profits will depend on the number of units of the storable shoppers buy at the sale price, which in turn depends on shoppers' storable good inventory holdings. In Section II.A, we noted that for certain parameter values, shoppers will rationally believe that if $\min_j \{P_{S,t}^j\} \le s_L \delta^{m-1+I_{t-1}}$, then there will not be a sale for the next M + 1 - I_{t-1} periods. As such, consumers will purchase M + 1 - I_{t-1} units whenever $\min_j \{P_{S,t}^j\} \le \delta^M s_L$. Conditions (1)-(4), stated below, provide sufficient conditions for these beliefs to hold in equilibrium.

In general, when she has an inventory of I_{t-1}, shopper k's maximum willingness to pay for the mth unit is $P_{S,t}^j \le s_L \delta^{m-1+I_{t-1}}$ since shoppers will not be consuming the m + I_{t-1} unit until period

$t + m - 1 + I_{t-1}$ This implies that, conditional on an initial inventory of I_{t-1}, the revenue a firm can obtain from a shopper $(mP^j_{S,t})$ is less than or equal to $s_L \delta^{m+I_{t-1}-1}$. We assume that

Condition (1): $m \, \delta^{m+I_{t-1}-1} s_L$ is strictly increasing in m for all $m \leq M+1- I_{t-1,}$ [12] and

Condition (2): $\dfrac{\gamma(s_H + P^j_{P,t})}{N} > \dfrac{\gamma(s_L + P^j_{P,t})}{N} + (1-\gamma)(\delta^M s_L + P^j_{P,t})$ for all $P^j_{P,t} \in (0,\beta)$.

The first condition means that potential revenues from a sale are maximized at $P^j_{S,t} = \delta^M s_L$.

The second condition means that a sale on the storable will not be profitable if $I_{t-1} = M$ (note that all shoppers buy at most one unit of the storable when $I_{t-1} = M$). Condition (2) implies that a necessary condition for retailers to choose to put the storable on sale is $I_{t-1} < M$. This in turn implies that having a sale on both goods is always less profitable than having a sale on only one good, as shown in Proposition 3.

Proposition 3: If conditions (1) and (2) hold, then it is not profitable to place both the perishable and the storable on sale in the same period, (i.e., retailer j will not set $P^j_{S,t} < s_L$ and $P^j_{P,t} < \beta$).

Proof: First note that it is never profit-maximizing for a retailer to set $P^j_{S,t}$ between $\delta^M s_L$ and s_H. A $P^j_{S,t}$ between s_L and s_H generates zero surplus on the storable to shoppers, and hence zero probability of attracting shoppers, but yields lower retailer's profits from loyals than $P^j_{S,t} = s_H$. For values of $P^j_{S,t} \leq s_L$, the profitability of a sale depends on I_{t-1}. If $I_{t-1} = M$, then shoppers will buy one unit or less when the storable is on sale, and by condition (2), retailers will earn more by charging $P^j_{S,t} = s_H$ and $P^j_{P,t} = \beta$. If $I_{t-1} < M$, retailers might choose $P^j_{S,t} \leq s_L$. However, retailers would never choose a $P^j_{S,t}$ between $\delta^M s_L$ and s_L, since by condition (1) a $P^j_{S,t}$ between $\delta^M s_L$ and s_L yields lower revenue than charging $\delta^M s_L$. Finally, if $P^j_{S,t} \leq \delta^M s_L$ and $I_{t-1} < M$, then $P^j_{P,t} < \beta$ is not profit maximizing. The reason is that if $P^j_{S,t} \leq \delta^M s_L$ and $I_{t-1} < M$, then shoppers all purchase $M + 1 - I_{t-1}$

---

[12]   In the context of supermarket purchases this relationship is plausible; "periods" should be thought of as weeks, so that δ would be close to 1, and the maximal number of weeks of storage (M) would be a relatively small (<10) number.

(> 1) units, and an increase of ϵ in $P_{P,t}^{j}$ accompanied by a decrease in $P_{P,t}^{j}$ of $\epsilon/(M + 1 - I_{t-1})$ increases retailer j's profits from loyals without lowering Ψ, or his profit from shoppers, conditional on offering the highest Ψ. This implies that whenever $P_{S,t}^{j} \leq \delta^{M} s_{L}$ the retailer will set $P_{P,t}^{j} = \beta$. Hence, having only one good on sale dominates having both on sale (i.e., $P_{P,t}^{j} < \beta$ and $P_{S,t}^{j} \leq s_{L}$).⊠

The intuition behind Proposition 3 is that the cost of offering any given level of consumer surplus ($\Psi_{j,t}$) to shoppers is the foregone profits that could be obtained by selling to loyals only. For any given $\Psi_{j,t}$, retailer j wishes to offer it in a way that minimizes this loss. Hence, if $P_{S,t}^{j} \leq \delta^{M} s_{L}$ and $P_{P,t}^{j} < \beta$, then reducing $P_{S,t}^{j}$ by $\epsilon/(M + 1 - I_{t-1})$, and increasing $P_{P,t}^{j}$ by ϵ will increase profits from store-loyals, who only buy one unit of each good, without lowering $\Psi_{j,t}$ (assuming $I_{t-1} < M$).

In combination with Proposition 1, Proposition 3 implies that *exactly* one product will be on sale at each point in time. This has implications for pricing dynamics. For example, price movements for the perishable and non-perishable goods should be negatively correlated at each retailer. Specifically, in the symmetric equilibrium, if the storable good price changes, the perishable price will move in the opposite direction.[13]

Having shown that every retailer puts exactly one product on sale each period, we next address the question of which product will be on sale. A necessary condition for a retailer to choose to put a product on sale is that expected profits are at least equal to $\dfrac{\gamma(s_{H} + \beta)}{N}$. In addition, a necessary condition for shoppers to buy $M + 1 - I_{t-1}$ units of the storable is that $P_{S,t}^{j} \leq s_{L}\delta^{M}$. Finally, condition (1) implies that revenue from having a sale on the storable is

---

[13] The implication that no more than one product will be on sale at any point in time derives in part from the assumption that shoppers necessarily visit no more than one retailer in each period. As we discuss in Section III, in a model in which shoppers can (at some cost) visit multiple retailers, equilibrium might consist of multiple goods being on sale.

maximized at $P_{S,t}^j = s_L \delta^M$. In combination, these conditions imply that a sale on the storable can only be profitable if:

$$\frac{\gamma(\delta^M s_L + \beta)}{N} + (1-\gamma)((M+1-I_{t-1})s_L \delta^M + \beta) \geq \frac{\gamma(s_H + \beta)}{N}.$$

We assume this condition is met for $I_{t-1} = 0$. That is, we assume condition (3) below.

$$\text{Condition (3)}: \qquad M+1 \geq \frac{\frac{\gamma}{N(1-\gamma)}(s_H - \delta^M s_L) - \beta}{\delta^M s_L} \equiv \mu$$

We also assume that a sale on the storable will not be profitable if $I_{t-1} \geq 1$, that is, if all shoppers purchased M or fewer units. This is equivalent to condition (4) below:

$$\text{Condition (4)}: \qquad M < \mu.$$

Thus, a necessary condition for any individual retailer to have a sale on the storable is that virtually all shoppers will buy M+1 units whenever it is on sale. Hence, from an individual shopper's perspective, this means that if conditions 1-4 hold, she anticipates that sales on the storable will only occur in periods in which other shoppers have zero inventory entering the period.

Formally, in each period, retailers simultaneously choose their prices, and then consumers simultaneously make their purchasing decisions based on those prices. Each consumer has measure zero, and views price as exogenous to her purchasing decision. If all shoppers have positive inventory entering period t, then condition (4) implies that no retailer will find it profitable to have a sale on the storable. Therefore, Proposition 1 implies that the perishable will be on sale whenever the state variable (I_{t-1}) is not zero. To summarize,

Proposition 4: If conditions (3) and (4) hold (M < μ < M+1) and I_{t-1} > 0, then $P_{P,t}^j < \beta$ and $P_{S,t}^j = s_H$ for all j.

Proposition 4 implies that, just as in the single-product model discussed above, the storable will be at a single "regular" level most of the time, since a necessary condition for

15

retailers to choose $P^j_{S,t} < s_H$ is that $I_{t-1} = 0$. Perishable prices will be the same as in the Varian model when $I_{t-1} > 0$. In this case the surplus that retailer j offers consumers is $\Psi_{j,t} = \beta - P^j_{P,t}$.

When $I_{t-1} = 0$ retailer j could place the perishable or the storable on sale. If retailer j places the perishable on sale, the surplus he offers is $\Psi_{j,t} = \beta - P^j_{P,t}$. In general, it is not possible to derive a closed form for $\Psi_{j,t}$ if retailer j places the storable is on sale. We can, however, derive a closed form for the surplus retailer j offers consumers in a special case. Assume that shopper k enters period t with her inventory $I_{t-1} = 0$, observes $\min_j (P^j_{S,t}) \leq \delta^M s_L$ and also believes that $\min_j (P^j_{S,t})$ will be equal to s_H for periods t+1 through M+t. In this case, it will be rational for her to buy M+1 units of the storable in period t if she buys from retailer j. If she were to buy m < M+1 units, she would expect to receive zero surplus on the storable in each period t+ τ, where $\tau \in (m, M)$, rather than $\delta^\tau s_L - P^j_{S,t}$ in each. Hence, when her $I_{t-1} = 0$, buying M+1 units if she visits retailer j is individually rational for shopper k when j storable price is below $\delta^M s_L$. This means that when the storable is on sale, we have a closed-form expression for $\Psi_{j,t}$:

$$\Psi_{j,t} = \sum_{\tau=0}^{M} \delta^t s_L - (M+1)P^j_{S,t}$$

In the next subsection we will used these expressions for consumer surplus in deriving retailer's equilibrium pricing when $I_{t-1}=0$. In particular, we show that when $I_{t-1}=0$ retailers may place either the perishable or storable product on sale depending on how much surplus they choose to offer consumers.

C. Equilibrium Pricing

The previous subsection showed that equilibrium when $I_{t-1} > 0$ is characterized by sales on the perishable only. Hence, if shoppers purchase more than one unit of the storable when it is on sale, then a sale on the storable is never followed by another sale on the storable.

Our next result establishes that either good may be on sale when $I_{t-1} = 0$. From Proposition 1 we know that firms play a mixed strategy with respect to the amount of surplus ($\Psi_{j,t}$) offered. The choice of whether to place the storable or perishable on sale to generate a given Ψ when $I_{t-1} = 0$ depends on the level of $\Psi_{j,t}$ the retailer chooses to offer shoppers. Lemma 1 defines a break-even consumer surplus, denoted $\overline{\Psi}$, such that the most profitable way to offer small Ψ (i.e., $\Psi < \overline{\Psi}$) is to put the perishable on sale, and to put the storable on sale when offering large Ψ. The intuition for this result is that offering any surplus to shoppers requires reducing profits from loyals. Retailers choose prices in such a way as to minimize the reduction in profits from loyals for any given Ψ. For small amounts of Ψ, setting $P_{P,t}^{j}$ less than β leads to a smaller reduction in profits from loyals than setting $P_{S,t}^{j}$ below s_L (since offering Ψ by reducing $P_{S,t}^{j}$ requires a price reduction of at least s_H-s_L) to obtain that Ψ, so that it will be more profitable to offer small Ψ by lowering $P_{P,t}^{j}$. Conversely, for large amounts of Ψ, it can be more profitable to lower $P_{S,t}^{j}$ in order to generate a given Ψ.

As long as the upper support of $G(\Psi)$ is greater than $\overline{\Psi}$, then both goods will be on sale with a positive probability when $I_{t-1} = 0$ (the condition under which this inequality holds is provided in part c of Lemma 1). [14] Lemma 1 solves for $\overline{\Psi}$ and provides the basis for determining the distribution function for $\Psi_{j,t}$.

Lemma 1: Suppose conditions (3) and (4) hold, $I_{t-1} = 0$ and let

$$\overline{\Psi} = \left(\frac{M+1}{M}\right)\left(s_H - \frac{\sum_{\tau=0}^{M}\delta^{\tau}s_L}{M+1} - \left(\frac{N(1-\gamma)}{\gamma}\right)\Pr(\overline{\Psi})\sum_{\tau=0}^{M}\delta^{\tau}s_L\right)$$

---

[14]   We assume this inequality holds in what follows. If this inequality is not satisfied, then only the perishable will be on sale. Since we want to explain the observed pattern of sale behavior, we assume conditions hold that make a sale on the storable profitable.

Then, if shoppers believe that $\min_j (P_{S,t}^j)$ will be equal to s_H for periods t+1 through M+t,

a. $\overline{\Psi} > 0$,

b. $\pi_P (\Psi_{j,t}) > \pi_S (\Psi_{j,t})$ for all $\Psi_{j,t} < \overline{\Psi}$,

c. If $\sum_{\tau=0}^{M} \delta^\tau s_L - (M+1)\underline{P}_S > \overline{\Psi}$ then to offer surplus $\Psi_{j,t}$, it will be more profitable to put the

storable on sale than the perishable for $\Psi_{j,t}$ such that $\sum_{\tau=0}^{M} \delta^\tau s_L - (M+1)\underline{P}_S > \Psi_{j,t} > \overline{\Psi}$, where

$$\underline{P}_S = \frac{\gamma s_H - N(1-\gamma)\beta}{\gamma + N (1-\gamma) (M+1)}$$ (i.e., the lowest price a retailer could profitable charge for

the storable).

Proof: See Appendix A.

Lemma 1 indicates that in the symmetric equilibrium $\overline{\Psi}$ is always positive. Since the

lower support of $G(\Psi)$ is zero, this means that when $I_{t-1} = 0$, it will be profit maximizing for

the retailer to discount the perishable to generate small levels of consumer surplus ($\Psi_{j,t} < \overline{\Psi}$).

Because we assume that the upper support of $G(\Psi)$ is greater than $\overline{\Psi}$, the retailer will place the

storable on sale when it offers a large amount of consumer surplus to shoppers ($\psi_{j,t} > \overline{\psi}$).

One practical implication of Lemma 1 is that the maximum discount offered on the

perishable will be smaller when $I_{t-1} = 0$. That is, the lowest price that will be observed for the

perishable when $I_{t-1} = 0$ is $\beta - \overline{\Psi}$, which is less than the maximum discount offered when $I_{t-1} > 0$

(which is $\beta[1-1/(\gamma+N(1-\gamma))]$). A related implication concerns the cross-sectional relationship

between characteristics of the storable and price discounts. We would expect a consumer's

maximum inventory holdings of a good (M) to vary across storable goods. For example,

because soda is much bulkier than canned tuna, we would expect the costs of storing soda to

18

exceed those of storing tuna, and hence consumers' capacity to store tuna would be greater than for soda; that is $M_{tuna} > M_{soda}$. This implies that consumers will stock out of goods like soda more frequently than items like tuna. Thus, storable products with lower maximum inventory holdings (M) will have more frequent sales. Another, more subtle implication of Lemma 1 concerns the perishable price distribution. Since $\overline{\Psi}$ is decreasing in M, the maximum discount on the *perishable* product when $I_{t-1} = 0$ is decreasing in M. Consequently, Lemma 1 implies that the maximum possible discount on the perishable falls as the storage costs of the storable falls.

Another implication of Lemma 1.C is that whenever the storable is on sale, the surplus shoppers receive from buying the storable will be greater than the surplus they could get from any retailer who offers has a sale on the perishable. These results allows us to derive the symmetric equilibrium when $\mathbf{I_{t-1}} = 0$.

Proposition 5: If $M < \mu < M+1$, and $\mathbf{I_{t-1}} = 0$, then an equilibrium exists in which all shoppers buy M+1 units of the storable at $\min_{j} \{P_{S,t}^{j}\}$, as long as $\min\{P_{S,t}^{j}\} \leq \delta^{M} s_{L}$. Retailers set $P_{S,t}^{j} \leq \delta^{M} s_{L}$ with a positive probability.

Proof: By Proposition 4, all agents know that there will no sales on the storable in any period in which $\mathbf{I_{t-1}} > 0$. It follows that if $\min\{P_{S,t}^{j}\} \leq \delta^{M} s_{L}$, and shopper k believes that all other shoppers will buy M+1 units in period t, then it would be optimal for her to buy M+1 units as well, as long as

$$\sum_{\tau=0}^{M} \delta^{\tau} s_{L} - (M+1) \min_{j} (P_{S,t}^{j}) \geq \beta - \min_{j'} (P_{P,t}^{j'})$$ (i.e., surplus on the storable exceeds the maximum possible surplus on the perishable). Lemma 1.C implies this condition will hold whenever the storable in on sale. Hence, no shopper has an incentive to deviate from a strategy of buying M+1 units whenever $P_{S,t}^{j} \leq \delta^{M} s_{L}$. As such, the belief that $P_{S,\tau}^{j} = s_{H}$ for all j for $\tau \in (t+1, M+1)$ is validated in equilibrium.

Given that all shoppers will buy M+1 units as long as $P_{S,t}^j \leq \delta^M s_L$, retailers will find it profitable to offer $P_{S,t}^j \leq \delta^M s_L$ when $I_{t-1} = 0$. To see why, assume $I_{t-1} = 0$, and to the contrary, that no retailer is offering $P_{S,t}^j \leq \delta^M s_L$. Then retailer j's profit from setting $P_{S,t}^j \leq \delta^M s_L$ is

$$\frac{\gamma(\delta^M s_L + \beta)}{N} + (1-\gamma)((M+1)s_L \delta^M + \beta)$$

which is greater than the profits from a sale on the perishable, by condition (3). Therefore, offering a sale would be profitable, contradicting the premise that having a sale on the storable yields lowers profits. It follows that in the symmetric equilibrium, all retailers set $P_{S,t}^j \leq \delta^M s_L$ with a positive probability if $I_{t-1} = 0$. ∎

Proposition 5 shows that there is an equilibrium in which sales on the storable are profitable if $I_{t-1} = 0$, and when they occur shoppers will purchase M+1 units. Since each retailer puts at least one product on sale each period (Proposition 1), Lemma 1 implies that the probability of a sale on the perishable when $I_{t-1} = 0$ is positive as well. Propositions 4 and 5, along with Lemma 1, characterize pricing behavior for the two relevant states; $I_{t-1} = 0$, and $I_{t-1} > 0$. Hence, the behavior described in these results represents the Markov perfect symmetric equilibrium.

Finally, Lemma 1.C also implies that when $I_{t-1} = 0$, $G(\Psi)$ can be decomposed into two cumulative distribution functions; $G(\Psi) = 1 - F_S(P_S)$ for $\Psi_{j,t} \geq \bar{\bar{\Psi}}$ and

$$G(\Psi) = (1 - F_S(\sum_{\tau=0}^{M} \delta^t s_L - \bar{\bar{\Psi}}))(1 - F_P(P_P)) \text{ for } \Psi_{j,t} < \bar{\bar{\Psi}}.$$ Proposition 6 derives the closed-form

expressions for the two distribution functions in the two states.

Proposition 6. Let $F_S(P_S)$ be the distribution of storable prices and $F_P(P_P)$ be the distribution of perishable prices in the symmetric equilibrium. Then, if $I_{t-1} = 0$, $M < \mu < M+1$, and

$$\sum_{\tau=0}^{M} \delta^\tau s_L - (M+1)\underline{P}_S > \bar{\bar{\Psi}},$$

a. then retailer j puts the storable on sale with probability $\Omega = 1 - G(\overline{\Psi})$.

$$\Omega = 1 - \left[\frac{\frac{\gamma}{N}(s_H - P_S(\overline{\Psi}))}{(1-\gamma)[(M+1)P_S(\overline{\Psi}) + \beta]} \right]^{\frac{1}{N-1}}$$

where $P_S(\overline{\Psi}) = \dfrac{(\sum_{\tau=0}^{M} \delta^{\tau} s_L - \overline{\Psi})}{M+1}$. When the storable is on sale, $P_P = \beta$. This implies that the

cumulative distribution function for P_S is

$$\left[\begin{array}{ll} 1 - \left[\dfrac{\gamma(s_H - P_S)}{N(1-\gamma)[(M+1)P_S + \beta]} \right]^{\frac{1}{N-1}} & \text{for } P_S \in [\underline{P}_S, \dfrac{\sum_{\tau=0}^{M} \delta^{\tau} s_L - \overline{\Psi}}{M+1}], \\[3em] \Omega & \text{for } P_S \in [\dfrac{\sum_{\tau=0}^{M} \delta^{\tau} s_L - \overline{\Psi}}{M+1}, s_H] \\[3em] 1 & \text{for } P_S = s_H \end{array} \right.$$

b. With probability $1 - \Omega$ retailer j sets $P_S = s_H$, and chooses P_P according to the distribution

function $F_P(P_P) = 1 - [\dfrac{(\beta - P_P)\gamma}{N(1-\gamma)P_P}]^{\frac{1}{N-1}}(1-\Omega)^{-1}$.

for $P_P \in (\beta/(\gamma+N(1-\gamma)), \beta - \overline{\Psi})$.

Proof: See Appendix A.

Proposition 6 shows that when $I_{t-1} = 0$, each retailer randomizes over which good to put on sale, and chooses a price for that good from an atomless distribution. If all retailers choose to put the perishable on sale in period t, then I_t will equal 0, and the ex-ante distribution of Ψ in period t+1 will be identical to the distribution in period t. Conversely, if at least one retailer has a sale on the storable in period t, then the perishable will be on sale, and the storable price will be s_H for the next M or more periods.

Proposition 6 demonstrates the importance of modeling the multiproduct aspect of a retailer's offerings - prices for both goods are different than they would be if the goods were sold by a single-product retailer in the same environment (i.e., with shoppers and store-loyals). In particular, the perishable price distribution has a mass point (at $P_P = \beta$), and the storable price distribution is decreasing in the price of the perishable good, with the expected storable price falling as the expected price of the perishable good rises (to see this, note that F_S is increasing in β, and the single-product models are equivalent to $\beta = 0$).[15] The model also generalizes Varian's result that competition results in prices that are drawn from an atomless distribution. In the multiproduct environment, the analogue to this result is the proposition that $\Psi_{j,t}$ is chosen from an atomless distribution.

Further, the model explains three of the features of the observed price distributions described in the introduction. First, while the distribution of $\Psi_{j,t}$ has no mass points, both the perishable and storable price distributions derived in Proposition 6 have mass points (at β and s_H respectively), consistent with the large modes found in the empirical distributions. Second,

---

[15]   That is, the profit that can be earned from each shopper when $P_S < \delta^M s_L$ includes both profit from the storable (as in the single-product case) and profit from the perishable (β). Hence, more intense competition on the storable arises in the multiproduct case.

storable good prices will be at non-modal levels for shorter periods of time than at modal levels.[16]

Finally, the model has several additional implications for price distributions. For example, it implies that a storable is more likely to have the same price in consecutive periods than a perishable, and conditional on a price reduction occurring, the average change will be larger for the storable. To see this last point, note that the maximal possible discount off the regular perishable price will be $\beta - \beta\gamma/(\gamma+N(1-\gamma)) = N\beta(1-\gamma)/(\gamma+N(1-\gamma))$, while the minimum possible discount on the storable is $s_H - \delta^M s_L$ which is greater than $N\beta(1-\gamma)/\gamma$ (by the condition that $\mu > M$) and this in turn is greater than $N\beta(1-\gamma)/(\gamma+N(1-\gamma))$.

Another impliction concerns the relationship between M and the size and frequency of discounts. As noted above, higher M goods will have less frequent sales. In addition, the lower bound on the distribution of storable price ($\underline{P}_S$) is decreasing in M, so that larger discounts will be observed on low storage-cost products. Casual empiricism is consistent with the former prediction. Bulky products that are consumed frequently, such as soft drinks, go on sale frequently. Products for which it is feasible to store a sufficient quantity to cover demand for a long period of time, such as laundry detergent, go on sale less frequently. Hendel and Nevo's finding that soft-drinks are discounted much more frequently than laundry detergent supports this premise.[17]

III. Discussion

Our model provides an explanation for retail price variation that comports with the empirical evidence. By necessity, the model simplifies much of the complexity facing retailers to draw its conclusions. In this section we highlight a few of the model's key assumptions and examine their relationship to observed retailer and consumer behavior.

---

[16]   Generalizing the model to allow reservation values or costs to vary over time, the logic of the model suggests that prices below the mode will be more common than prices above it.

[17]   Hendel and Nevo find that soft drinks are discounted at least 5% from its regular price about twice as frequently as for laundry detergent.

Like the previous literature developed to explain retail sales, our model relies on assumptions of consumer heterogeneity. Recent empirical work is consistent with our assumptions regarding consumer heterogeneity with respect to shopping costs and storage costs. Specifically, Pesendorfer finds considerable inter-household variation in search behavior. Within the three-year period Pesendorfer studied, 20% of consumers visited the same store at least 95% of the time, while 20% of consumers visited three different stores at least 20% of the time. We also assume valuations of the storable good, search costs and storage (or waiting) costs are positively correlated. This could reflect the premise that high-income consumers are likely to have higher reservation values for many goods, and due to a higher shadow value of time, lower willingness to invest in learning about prices and taking steps to take advantage of that knowledge. Consistent with this premise, Hendel and Nevo find that a household's responsiveness to a sale is decreasing in household income, with large inter-household differences in the percentage of units purchased on discount.

Our assumption that there is more variation in consumers' reservation values for storable than perishables goods is also plausible. Storable goods typically have more manufacturer value-added than perishables (e.g., breakfast cereal as compared to milk). Products with considerable manufacturer value-added will typically be those for which brand names are important. Theory suggests that brand names will be more valuable for consumers who view search as particularly costly (see, e.g., Klein and Leffler, 1981, and Ward and Lee, 1999, for recent evidence), which implies greater heterogeneity in reservation values for branded products than commodities. The fact that supermarkets typically carry a single product in many perishable categories, (e.g., produce, fluid milk, ground beef), while carrying multiple versions in the storable categories suggests that heterogeneity in consumer valuations of products is more important for storable than perishable products.

We make strong assumptions about the information available to consumers and retailers in making their shopping and pricing decisions, respectively. Consumers are assumed to know the prices of all goods at all retailers, and retailers are assumed to know the inventory holdings of shoppers. While not literally true, we think that the information available to consumers and retailers allows them to make decisions that closely approximate those they would make if fully informed.

Specifically, the typical supermarket sells over 35,000 items, and consumers cannot possibly know all of the prices that will be relevant to their decision-making without visiting each retailer, or having retailers list all their prices in a public forum. As a practical matter, it is costly for consumers to visit retailers and for retailers to advertise their prices, so that consumers will be less than fully informed about prices. Nevertheless, as Lal and Matutes (L&M, 1994) show, even without knowledge of every price, consumers can be well informed about the surplus they will receive at each retailer. L&M show that when retailers advertise a subset of prices, consumers can draw correct inferences about the remaining prices, and therefore calculate the surplus they will receive that each retailer. Similarly, in our model, consumer would correctly infer the price of any non-sale item.

The empirical counterpart to the assumption that retailers advertise a subset of their products is the advertising circular that most chain supermarkets in the U.S. provide to virtually all consumers in a metropolitan area.[18] The circular informs consumers about the prices of the several hundred products that will be sold at below the regular price during the upcoming week. This information, combined with their knowledge of regular prices (recall that most goods are at their regular level most of the time), allows consumers to compare surplus across retailers before deciding where to shop, as in the L&M model.

In a model in which consumers only visit one retailer per period, retailers would never place more than one perishable good on sale at one time. By allowing consumers to, at some cost, visit multiple retailers in the same period, the L&M model provides an explanation for why multiple perishable goods may be on sale in the same week.[19] In their model, total advertising costs are increasing in the number of goods advertised, so that the retailer would prefer to guarantee surplus through a small number of goods. However, if a small number of goods are on sale at a deep discount at each retailer and the items are different across retailers, then shoppers

---

[18]   The obvious exception to this pattern is WalMart, now the U.S.'s largest retailer. WalMart's strategy is to charge low everyday prices and avoid sales. WalMart arguably has very different pricing incentives than other food retailers because so much of its product selection contains consumer durables, e.g., tires, clothing, hardware, and consumer electronics.

[19]   Hosken and Reiffen (2001) also consider the effect of allowing consumers to shop at more than one retail outlet in a period.

could "cream skim"; visiting multiple retailers and buying only low-priced goods. To avoid this, in the L&M equilibrium, retailers choose to spread the aggregate discount across enough goods to mitigate the cream skimming potential.

While the L&M model explains the number of items listed in the circular, it is static and consequently does not explain why the composition of items in a circular changes from week to week. Our model can form a basis for understanding this practice. When a retailer carries multiple storable goods with different inventory patterns (i.e., different M), each good will have its own sale frequency. Hence, the number and identity of storables on sale will change from week to week. Extending the logic of Proposition 3 to this environment, this suggests that in weeks in which the number of storables that are appropriate for putting on sale is low (i.e., consumer inventories are high), the number of perishables on sale will increase.

We also assume that all shoppers have identical inventory holdings, and that the time since the last sale on a storable product is a sufficient statistic for the level of that inventory. Neither of these assumptions is literally true. Even among individuals who do inventory storables, there will be heterogeneity in inventory behavior due to differential storage costs. Such heterogencity will result in more complex pricing variation than is modeled here. However, retailers likely have reasonably accurate information about average inventory. Because retailers communicate sale prices through weekly circulars, it is not costly for a retailer to monitor rivals' recent sale behavior. This information, along with their own recent pricing history and information on average consumer consumption behavior, can allow retailers to develop reasonable expectations about average consumer inventory holdings.

IV. Conclusion

With the increasing availability of high-quality data on retail prices and quantities, economists (as well as marketing professionals and others) have enthusiastically begun to estimate economic magnitudes, such as demand elasticities. It is well understood that identifying these magnitudes requires variation in some independent variable, such as price. What is perhaps less well appreciated is the relevance of the source of this variation. Empirical evidence suggests that sales account for 25-50% of the annual price variation for popular categories of grocery products. Because these temporary reductions are such an important source of price variation, understanding why these changes occur is critical to interpreting econometric estimates which use this data.

Our model implies that the multiproduct aspect of a supermarket's offerings influences how its prices change over time. Consumers who are price-sensitive shoppers likely examine weekly supermarket circulars and choose the retailer offering the best (utility maximizing) set of prices for that consumer. This implies that prices of other goods sold by a retailer will influence the quantity it sells of each good. In our highly stylized model, retailers will achieve maximal unit sales of the perishable when they have the lowest price for the storable, and when this occurs the retailer's perishable price will also be at its maximum value. Thus, the model suggests that there can be a positive relationship between observed sales of the perishable and its price. Consequently, a researcher attempting to estimate a demand curve for a perishable product (e.g., milk) using store or chain level data may well estimate an upward sloping demand curve. The potential bias results because of the difficulty in distinguishing between movements of a store's demand curve (from having more customers in the store) versus movements along a demand curve (resulting from exogenous changes in price). We suspect this aggregation problem could be most severe for perishable products purchased frequently.

For this reason, it is likely that more accurate estimates of demand elasticities can be obtained using individual household-level data. The advantage of household level estimation is that once an individual chooses a retailer, his or her choice of how many units of each perishable to buy depends only on the prices at that retailer during that week.

More generally, we view the multiproduct nature of consumers' purchases as an important aspect of the demand facing retailers. The model presented here shows how this aspect makes the two-product retailer choose different prices than two single-product retailers. Of course, goods sold by a single retailer differ in ways other than those modeled here, and consequently retailers have even richer pricing alternatives than our model suggests. Future research that analyzes the impact of these differences across products (e.g., differences in likelihood of purchase) would help develop a more complete understanding of the observed pricing behavior of multiproduct retailers.

References

Aguirregabira, Victor (1999) "The Dynamic Markups and Inventories in Retailing Firms," *Review of Economic Studies*; 66, pp.275-308.

Chevalier, Judith, Anil Kashyap, and Peter Rossi (2003) "Why Don't Prices Rise During Periods of Peak Demand? Evidence from Scanner Data," *American Economic Review*; 93, pp.15-37

Conlisk, John, Eitan Gerstner, and Joel Sobel (1984) "Cyclic Pricing by a Durable Goods Monopolist," *Quarterly Journal of Economics;* 99, pp. 489-505

DeGraba, Patrick (2006) "The Loss Leader is a Turkey: Targeted Discounts from Multi-product Competitors," *International Journal of Industrial Organization*; 24, pp.613-628

Dutta, Shantanu, Mark Bergen, and Daniel Levy (2002) "Price Flexibility in channels of Distribution: Evidence from Scanner Data," *Journal of Economic Dynamics & Control*; 26, pp. 1845-00.

Hendal, Igal, and Aviv Nevo "Sales and Consumer Inventory," *Rand Journal of Economics*, forthcoming.

Hong, Pilky, R. Preston McAfee, and Ashish Nayyar (2002) "Equilibrium Price Dispersion with Consumer Inventories" *Journal of Economic Theory*; 105, pp. 503-517.

Hosken, Daniel and David Reiffen (2001) "Multiproduct Retailers and the Sale Phenomenon," *Agribusiness*; 17, pp.115-137

___ (2004a) "Patterns of Retail Price Variation," *RAND Journal of Economics*; 35, pp. 128-146.

___ (2004b) "How do Retailers Determine Sale Products: Evidence from Store-Level Data," *Journal of Consumer Policy*; 27, pp.141-177.

Klein, Benjamin and Keith Leffler (1981) "The Role of Market Forces in Assuring Contractual Performance," *Journal of Political Economy*; 89, pp. 615-41.

MacDonald, James (2000) "Demand, Information, and Competition: Why Do Food Prices Fall at Seasonal Demand Peaks?," *Journal of Industrial Economics*; 48, pp.27-45.

Lal, Rajiv and Carmen Matutes (1989) "Price Competition in Duopoly Markets," *RAND Journal of Economics*; 20, pp. 526-37.

___ (1994) "Retail Pricing and Advertising Strategies," *Journal of Business*; 67, pp. 345-70

Levy, Daniel, Mark Bergen, Shantanu Dutta, and Robert Venable (1997) "The Magnitude of Menu Costs: Direct Evidence from Large U.S. Supermarket Chains," *Quarterly Journal of Economics*; 112, pp. 791-825

Pashigian, B. Peter (1988) "Demand Uncertainty and Sales: A Study of Fashion and Markdown Pricing," *American Economic Review;* 78, pp. 936-53.

___ and Brian Bowen (1991) "Why are Products Sold on Sales?: Explanations of Pricing Regularities," *Quarterly Journal of Economics*; 106, pp.1014-1038.

Pesendorfer, Martin (2002) "Retail Sales: A Study of Pricing Behavior in Super Markets," *Journal of Business;* 75, pp.33-66

Sobel, Joel (1984) "The Timing of Sales," *Review of Economic Studies*; 51, pp. 353-68.

Varian, Hal R. (1980) "A Model of Sales," *American Economic Review*; 70, pp. 651-9.

Ward, Michael R. and Lee, Michael J. (2000) "Internet Shopping, Consumer Search and Product Branding," *Journal of Product and Brand Management*; 9, pp. 6-18.

Warner, Elizabeth J. and Robert B. Barsky (1995) "The Timing and Magnitude of Retail Store Markdowns: Evidence from Weekends and Holiday," *Quarterly Journal of Economics*; 110, pp. 321-52.

Appendix A

To prove Proposition 1, first note that when all shoppers begin a period with the same inventory, they all will receive the same Ψ from any given set of prices. Hence, Ψ is unambiguously defined in this case. We can therefore define $\mathbf{P(\Psi)}$ as the set of (P_{Pt}, P_{St}) that yield maximal profits among the set of prices that result in surplus Ψ. That is, while there are multiple pairs of P_{Pt} and P_{St} that yield any given level of surplus, the present value of expected profits could differ across these pairs. It follows that for any level of Ψ, firms will always choose to offer that Ψ by selecting prices in the set $\mathbf{P(\Psi)}$. Proposition 1 derives the properties of the symmetric distribution of Ψ, assuming prices are drawn from the set $\mathbf{P(\Psi)}$.

Proposition 1: The only symmetric equilibrium must feature all retailers playing a mixed strategy with respect to Ψ, $G(\Psi|I_{t-1})$, with the following features

A. has no mass points

B. a lower support of 0

Proof: To show these properties, I first show (in parts 1 and 2) that results A and B hold in any period in which all consumers have the same I_{t-1}, so that Ψ is unambiguously defined, since all will receive the same Ψ from any given set of prices. In section 3 of the proof, we show that all consumers do indeed start each period with the same I_{t-1}.

1. To show that there are no mass point, the proof proceeds by contradiction. Assume all consumers have the same I_{t-1}, and suppose the symmetric equilibrium distribution of Ψ is such that there is a Ψ, which we denote $\hat{\Psi}$ that has a positive probability (ϕ) of being offered. Note that there can be multiple combinations of P_{Pt} and P_{St} within $\mathbf{P}(\hat{\Psi})$ that yield surplus $\hat{\Psi}$.

Let $\hat{P}_{St}$ and $\hat{P}_{Pt}$ be one pair within $\mathbf{P}(\hat{\Psi})$, and let $\pi(P_{Pt}, P_{St})$ be a firm's current-period profits, conditional on it offering the highest Ψ, so that

$$\pi(P_{S,t}, P_{P,t}) = \frac{\gamma}{N}(P_{S,t} + P_{P,t}) + (1 - \gamma)(m(P_{S,t})P_{S,t} + P_{P,t})$$

where $m(P_{St})$ is the number of units of the storable purchased at P_{St}.

The number of points of positive mass in any probability distribution must be countable, so that we can find an arbitrarily small ϵ such that $\hat{\Psi} + \epsilon$ is offered with probability 0 in the proposed equilibrium. Suppose that firm i deviates from this proposed equilibrium by charging prices $\hat{P}_{St}$ and $\hat{P}_{Pt} - \varepsilon$. Conditional on firm i having the highest Ψ, this change does not lower expected future profits since it yields the same I_t as the pair $\hat{P}_{St}$ and $\hat{P}_{Pt}$. To see the effect on i's profits, note that since the present value of expected profits from all pairs of prices in $\mathbf{P}(\hat{\Psi})$ are identical, the change in i's expected profits from this deviation is equal to the change relative to charging $\hat{P}_{St}$ and $\hat{P}_{Pt}$. We see that such a deviation results in retailer i offering surplus $\hat{\Psi} + \epsilon$ with probability ϕ, and $\hat{\Psi}$ with probability 0. Compared to the pair $(\hat{P}_{St}, \hat{P}_{Pt})$, setting $P_{St} = \hat{P}_{St}$ and $P_{Pt} = \hat{P}_{Pt} - \varepsilon$ does not reduce i's future profits, and therefore the change in the present value of firm i's profits from that deviation is equal to the change in period t profits,

$$\Pr(\Psi_j < \hat{\Psi} + \varepsilon, \text{for all } j, \Psi_j \neq \hat{\Psi} \text{ for any } j)\pi(\hat{P}_{S,t}, \hat{P}_{P,t} - \varepsilon) - \Pr(\Psi_j < \hat{\Psi}, \text{for all } j)\pi(\hat{P}_{S,t}, \hat{P}_{P,t}) +$$

$$\Pr(\Psi_j > \hat{\Psi} + \varepsilon, \text{for some } j)\frac{\gamma}{N}(\hat{P}_{S,t} + \hat{P}_{P,t} - \varepsilon) - \Pr(\Psi_j > \hat{\Psi}, \text{for some } j)\frac{\gamma}{N}(\hat{P}_{S,t} + \hat{P}_{P,t})$$

$$\sum_{k=1,k\neq i}^{N} \Pr(\Psi_j \leq \hat{\Psi} + \varepsilon, \text{for all } j, \Psi_j = \hat{\Psi} \text{ for } k \text{ firms})\pi(\hat{P}_{S,t}, \hat{P}_{P,t} - \varepsilon) -$$

$$\sum_{k=1,k\neq i}^{N} \Pr(\Psi_j \leq \hat{\Psi} \text{ for all } j, \Psi_j = \hat{\Psi} \text{ for } k \text{ firms})[\frac{\gamma}{N}(\hat{P}_{P,t} + \hat{P}_{S,t}) + \frac{1-\gamma}{k+1}(\hat{P}_{P,t} + m(\hat{P}_{S,t})\hat{P}_{S,t})]$$

As ϵ approaches zero, the differences on the first two lines approach zero, while the difference on the last two lines becomes unambiguously positive. That is, there is a finite probability that k other firms offer surplus $\hat{\Psi}$, and when that occurs, firm i's profits in period t are higher by

$$\frac{1-\gamma}{k+1}[km(\hat{P}_{S,t})\hat{P}_{S,t} + k\hat{P}_{P,t} - (k+1)\varepsilon] - \frac{\gamma}{N}\varepsilon$$

which is positive for ϵ sufficiently small. Hence, for small ϵ, the change in profits is positive, contradicting the assumption of an equilibrium strategy.

2. To see that the lower support of $G(\Psi|I_{t-1})$ must be zero, again assume all consumers have the same I_{t-1}, and that the lower bound on the support of $G(\Psi|I_{t-1})$ was $\widetilde{\Psi} > 0$. Because there are no mass points in the distribution (by A), when the retailer offers surplus of $\widetilde{\Psi}$, the probability the retailer attracts shoppers is zero, so he winds up selling only to loyals. In order to generate $\widetilde{\Psi} >$ 0, at least one of the two prices would have to be set below shoppers' reservation values. However, the profits from selling only to loyals are higher and the likelihood of attracting shoppers the same when the retailer instead sets $P_{S,t}^{j} = s_H$ and $P_{P,t}^{j} = \beta$, which yields a surplus to shoppers of zero. Hence, the lower bound of the support of Ψ cannot have a value other than zero

3. The results in parts 1 and 2 hold in period 1, since all consumers have the same I_0. To see that they must hold in all periods, note that all shoppers must begin period 2 with the same inventory, since by 1 above, $G(\Psi|I_0)$ has no mass points. This is turn means that all shoppers bought from the same retailer in period 1 (the one offering the highest Ψ_{j1}), and all bought the same number of units of the storable. Hence, they all begin period 2 with the same I_1, and the analysis in parts 1 and 2 applies. By induction, in any period in which all shoppers begin with the same I_{t-1}, they will finish the period with the same I_t. ∎

Proposition 2:

A. Expected retailer profits from any $P_{S,t}^{j}$, $P_{P,t}^{j}$ in the equilibrium set of prices (i.e., every Ψ in the support of $G(\Psi|I_{t-1})$) are $\gamma(s_H + \beta)/N$, and independent of I_{t-1}.

B. $G(\Psi)$ represents a symmetric equilibrium.

Proof:

A. Proposition 1.B implies that setting prices $P_{S,t}^{j} = s_H$ and $P_{P,t}^{j} = \beta$, which yields a Ψ of 0, is within the support of $G(\Psi|I_{t-1})$ for all I_{t-1}. Proposition 1.A implies that this strategy yields profits of $\gamma(s_H + \beta)/N$ in every period. Hence, setting $P_{S,t}^{j} = s_H$ and $P_{P,t}^{j} = \beta$ in perpetuity is within the support of $G(\Psi|I_{t-1})$ regardless of the level of I_{t-1} in any period, and those prices yield a present value of expected future profits of $\gamma(s_H + \beta)/(1 - \delta)N$. It is also true that every strategy within $G(\Psi|I_{t-1})$ must yield the same present value of expected future profits. In particular, the present value of expected future profits at time t must be $\gamma(s_H + \beta)/(1 - \delta)N$, and the present value of expected future profits at time t+1 must also be $\gamma(s_H + \beta)/(1 - \delta)N$ for all Ψ in the support of $G(\Psi|I_t)$. Hence, profits in period t must be $\gamma(s_H + \beta)/(1 - \delta)N - \delta[\ \gamma(s_H + \beta)/(1 - \delta)N\ ] = \gamma(s_H + \beta)/N$ for any Ψ in the support of $G(\Psi|I_{t-1})$.

B. By A, all Ψ in the support of $G(\Psi)$ yield expected profits of $\gamma(s_H + \beta)/N$. To see that setting Ψ according to $G(\Psi)$ is undominated by any other Ψ, note the upper support of $G(\Psi)$ is defined as the Ψ such that, when a retailer offers Ψ, he attracts all shoppers with probability 1, so that his actual (realized) profits will be $\gamma(s_H + \beta)/N$. Hence, any offer of a Ψ greater than the upper support of $G(\Psi)$ will yield lower profits than offering a Ψ in the support (since it will involve lower price and the same unit sales). Since the lower bound on Ψ is zero by Proposition 1, it follows that setting a Ψ outside of the support of $G(\Psi)$ cannot increase a retailer's profit. Hence, $G(\Psi)$ (weakly) dominates any alternative. $\boxtimes$

Lemma 1: Suppose $I_{t-1} = 0$ and let

$$\overline{\Psi} = \left(\frac{M+1}{M}\right)\left(s_H - \frac{\sum_{\tau=0}^{M}\delta^\tau s_L}{M+1} - \left(\frac{N(1-\gamma)}{\gamma}\right)Pr(\overline{\Psi})\sum_{\tau=0}^{M}\delta^\tau s_L\right)$$

Then, if shoppers believe that $\min_{j}(P_{S,t}^j)$ will be equal to s_H for periods t+1 through M+t,

a. $\overline{\Psi} > 0$,

b. $\pi_P(\Psi_{j,t}) > \pi_S(\Psi_{j,t})$ for all $\Psi_{j,t} < \overline{\Psi}$,

c. If $\sum_{\tau=0}^{M}\delta^\tau s_L - (M+1)\underline{P}_S > \overline{\Psi}$ then will be more profitable to put the storable on sale than

the perishable for $\Psi_{j,t}$ such that $\sum_{\tau=0}^{M}\delta^\tau s_L - (M+1)\underline{P}_S > \Psi_{j,t} > \overline{\Psi}$, where

$$\underline{P}_S \ = \ \frac{\gamma s_H - N(1-\gamma)\beta}{\gamma + N\ (1-\gamma)\ (M+1)} \qquad \text{(i.e., the lowest price a retailer could profitable charge for}$$

the storable).

Proof:

a. $\overline{\Psi}$ must be non-negative, since $s_L < s_H$, and $Pr(0) = 0$. Define $\pi_P(\Psi)$ as retailer j's profits when it places only the perishable on sale, and offers surplus Ψ. Then

$$\pi_P = \frac{\gamma}{N}(\beta + s_H - \Psi) + (1-\gamma)Pr(\Psi_j)(\beta - \Psi)$$

Similarly, define $\pi_S(\Psi)$ as retailer j's profits when it places only the storable on sale, and offers surplus Ψ. W $I_{t-1} = 0$, a retailer who sets P_{St} less than $\delta^M s_L$ sells M+1 units if he has the highest Ψ, and hence the expected profits from putting the storable on sale to generate Ψ are

$$\pi_S = \frac{\gamma}{N}(\beta + \frac{\Sigma_{\tau=0}^{M}\delta^\tau s_L - \Psi_j}{M+1}) + (1-\gamma)Pr(\Psi_j)(\beta + \Sigma_{\tau=0}^{M}\delta^\tau s_L - \Psi_j)$$

To see that $\overline{\Psi}$ must be positive in equilibrium, note that $\lim_{\Psi \to 0}(\pi_P(\Psi)) = \gamma(s_H + \beta)/N >$ $\gamma(\Sigma^M\delta^\tau s_L /(M+1) + \beta)/N = \lim_{\Psi \to 0}(\pi_S(\Psi))$, where the inequality follows from the facts that $\delta < 1$ and $s_L < s_H$, so that $\Sigma^M\delta^\tau s_L < (M+1)\ s_H$. Hence, there must a range of Ψ for which $\pi_P(\Psi) > \pi_S(\Psi)$.

b. By Proposition 3, retailers will never put both products on sale. To determine which good is more profitable to put on sale for a given Ψ, first note that $\partial\pi_S(\Psi)/\partial\Psi > \partial\pi_P(\Psi)/\partial\Psi$, so that if $\pi_S(\Psi) > \pi_P(\Psi)$ for some $\hat{\Psi}$, π_S will be higher than π_P for all $\Psi > \hat{\Psi}$, and if $\pi_S(\Psi) < \pi_P(\Psi)$ for some $\hat{\Psi}$, π_S will be lower for all $\Psi < \hat{\Psi}$. Solving for the Ψ at which $\pi_S(\Psi) = \pi_P(\Psi)$ allows us to divide the set of all possible Ψ into two mutually exclusive sets; one in which lowering P_P is a more profitable way to generate Ψ and one in which lowering P_S is more profitable.

Specifically, $\pi_P(\Psi) > \pi_S(\Psi)$ if $\Psi < \overline{\Psi}$ where

$$\overline{\Psi} = \frac{M+1}{M}\left[(s_H - \frac{\sum_{\tau=0}^{M}\delta^\tau s_L}{M+1}) - \frac{N(1-\gamma)}{\gamma}(\Pr(\overline{\Psi})\sum_{\tau=0}^{M}\delta^\tau s_L)\right]$$

c. By Propositions 1-3, each retailer puts only one good on sale in any period. When the storable is on sale, the retailer's profit are $\pi_S(\Psi)$. Their profits must be at least as large as the retailer's profits from not having a sale, or $\gamma(\beta+s_H)/N$. Hence, even if the retailer knew for certain that he would attract all of the shoppers, the lowest storable price he would ever charge solves

$$\frac{\gamma}{N}(\beta + s_H) = \frac{\gamma}{N}(\beta + \underline{P}_S^j) + (1-\gamma)((M+1)\underline{P}_S^j + \beta)$$

or

$$\underline{P}_S = \frac{\gamma s_H - N(1-\gamma)\beta}{\gamma + N(1-\gamma)(M+1)}$$

Hence, the maximum possible surplus on the storable is if $\Sigma^M \delta^\tau s_L - (M+1)\underline{P}_S$. By construction, $\pi_S > \pi_P$ if $\Psi > \overline{\Psi}$. It follows that if $\Sigma^M \delta^\tau s_L - (M+1)\underline{P}_S > \overline{\Psi}$, then offering a sale on the storable yields higher profits to retailer j than having a sale on neither good, assuming no other retailer offers more than $\overline{\Psi}$ in surplus. ∎

Proof of Proposition 6: a. The previous results establish that for $I_{t-1} = 0$, Ψ is drawn from a continuous distribution with support $(0, \Sigma^M \delta^\tau s_L - (M+1)\underline{P}_S)$. In equilibrium, the profits each period from charging each price for which the density function is positive must be equal to the profits from charging $P_S = s_H$ and $P_P = \beta$, which are equal to $\gamma[\beta + s_H]/N$. To calculate $G(\Psi)$, note that by Proposition 3, retailer j will put at most one good on sale. Lemma 1 implies that if $\Sigma^M \delta^\tau s_L - (M+1)\underline{P}_S > \overline{\Psi}$, then whether P_S or P_P will be lowered in order to generate consumer surplus of Ψ depends on the magnitude of Ψ. For $\Psi > \overline{\Psi}$, Ψ is obtained by setting $P_S < \delta^M s_L$.

Given this result, in the symmetric equilibrium, when retailer j chooses a $\Psi > \overline{\Psi}$, the probability

35

that a rival offers more consumer surplus is equivalent to the probability the rival offers a lower P_S. Hence for $\Psi > \overline{\Psi}$, $G(\Psi) = 1 - F_S(P_S)$, where $F_S(P_S)$ is the common c.d.f. for P_S. To determine $F_S(P_S)$, note that any P_S for which the density function is positive must yield the same profits as can be obtained by not holding a sale. Hence, the distribution function for P_S, conditional on a sale occurring on the storable must solve

$$\frac{\gamma}{N}(s_H + \beta) = \frac{\gamma}{N}(P_S + \beta) + (1 - \gamma)[(M+1)P_S + \beta](1 - F_S(P_S))^{N-1} \qquad (A.1)$$

Solving for $F_S(P_S)$ yields

$$F_S(P_S) = 1 - \left[\frac{\frac{\gamma}{N}(s_H - P_S)}{(1 - \gamma)[(M+1)P_S + \beta]} \right]^{\frac{1}{N-1}}$$

The lower bound for the support is the lowest price the retailer could profitably charge for the storable item. Given Lemma 1, this price is

$$\underline{P}_S = \frac{\gamma s_H - N(1 - \gamma)\beta}{\gamma + N(1 - \gamma)(M+1)}$$

The highest P_S for which $G(\Psi) = 1 - F_1(P_S)$ corresponds to the Ψ for which it is equally profitable to have a sale on either product, or $P_S = (\Sigma^M \delta^\tau s_L - \overline{\Psi})/(M+1)$. By Lemma 6, for any $\Psi < \overline{\Psi}$, it will be more profitable to lower P_P rather than P_S, so that letting $\Omega \equiv F_S \left(\frac{\Sigma^M_{\tau=0} \delta^\tau s_L - \overline{\overline{\Psi}}}{M+1} \right)$,

we know that $F_S(P_S) = \Omega$ on the open interval $\left(\frac{\Sigma^M_{\tau=0} \delta^\tau s_L - \overline{\overline{\Psi}}}{M+1}, s_H \right)$, and $F_S(s_H) = 1$. By

Propositions 1 and 3 imply that when $P_S < s_L$, $P_P = \beta$.

b. From Proposition 1, we know that there is not a point mass at $\Psi = 0$, so that the perishable must be on sale whenever $P_S = s_H$. To solve for $F_P(P_P)$, the c.d.f. of P_P, first note that expected profits when the perishable is on sale at $P_P = \beta - \Psi$ are $\gamma(\beta - \Psi + s_H)/N + (1 - \gamma) G(\Psi)^{N-1}(\beta - \Psi)$. In equilibrium, this must equal the expected profits from not having a sale so that

$$G(\Psi) = \left(\frac{\Psi\gamma}{N(1-\gamma)(\beta-\Psi)}\right)^{\frac{1}{N-1}} \tag{A.2}$$

To relate $F_P(P_P)$ to $G(\Psi)$, note that if retailer j puts the perishable on sale, a rival might offer more consumer surplus either by putting the storable on sale, or by offering a lower perishable price. This means that the probability that any one rival offers more consumer surplus than retailer j is $1 - G(\Psi) = \Omega + (1 - \Omega)(F_P(P_P)) \Rightarrow G(\Psi) = (1 - \Omega)(1 - F_P(P_P))$. Using (A.2) this implies

$$F_P(P_P) = 1 - \left[\frac{(\beta-P_P)\gamma}{N(1-\gamma)P_P}\right]^{\frac{1}{N-1}}(1-\Omega)^{-1}. \blacksquare$$

Appendix B - Shoppers' Surplus Function

A shopper who enters period t with inventory, I_{t-1} seeks to maximize her utility, which is a function of her current and future consumption of the two goods. Shopper k's goal in time t is to pick the retailer (j) and make purchases of the perishable and storable to maximize the present discounted value of utility. The shopper's objective function at time t is equation (B.1) below.

$$V(\mathbf{I_{t-1}}, \mathbf{P_t}) = \max_{j} H_{jt} \qquad\qquad (B.1)$$

where $H_{jt} = \beta q_{P,t} + s_L q_{s,t} - P_{P,t}^j m_{P,t}^j - P_{S,t}^j m_{S,t}^j + \delta E(V(\mathbf{I}_t, \mathbf{P}_{t+1} | \mathbf{I_{t-1}}, \mathbf{P}_t))$. That is, H_{jt} is the

maximized value of the shopper's utility, conditional on her shopping at retailer j in period t. In equation (B.1) $\mathbf{I_{t-1}}$ and $\mathbf{P_t}$ (in bold) are vectors containing every shopper's inventory holdings of the storable good, and each retailer's prices (for both the storable and perishable goods) at time t. $P_{S,t}^j$ and $P_{P,t}^j$ are the two prices offered by retailer j at time t. All N pair of period t prices are

observable by the shopper, although future prices are not. H_{jt} depends on a shopper's own inventory of the storable good and contemporaneous and expected future prices. These future prices may, in turn, be a function of inventories held by others. Hence, we write V as a function of all observables, and indicate the relationship between future values and those observables (recalling that the vector $\mathbf{I_{t-1}}$ includes shopper k's inventory as well). $q_{S,t}$ and $q_{P,t} \in \{0,1\}$ are the shopper's consumption of the two goods at time t, and $m_{P,t}^j$ and $m_{S,t}^j$ are the purchases of the

perishable and storable goods from retailer j at time t. As noted in the text, when the consumer decides to make her purchases at retailer j, $m_{P,t}^j = q_{P,t}$; that is, perishable purchases at time t

must be consumed in time t. Thus, conditional on visiting retailer j, purchasing a unit of the perishable increases H_{jt} if and only if $P_{P,t}^j < \beta$. For the storable, $m_{S,t}^j = I_t - I_{t-1} + q_{S,t}$. To

simplify notation, we treat $m_{S,t}^j, m_{P,t}^j$ and I_{t-1} as integers, and suppress the retailer superscript on purchases (j).[20]

We define the function $\Psi_{jt} = \Psi_{jt}(\mathbf{I}_{t-1}, \mathbf{P}_t)$ as the difference between the H_{jt} associated

with optimal quantities when retailer j's prices are $P_{S,t}^j$ and $P_{P,t}^j$ in period t and H_{jt} *under the*

counterfactual in which a specific shopper (shopper k) was unable to shop anywhere in period t,
holding expected future prices constant. That is, the counterfactual H_{0t} is defined as:

$$H_{0t} = s_L + \delta E(V(\mathbf{I}_t', \mathbf{P}_{t+1} | \mathbf{I}_{t-1}, \mathbf{P}_t)) \text{ if } I_{t-1} \geq 0, \text{ and } H_{0t} = \delta E(V(\mathbf{I}_t', \mathbf{P}_{t+1} | \mathbf{I}_{t-1}, \mathbf{P}_t)) \text{ if } I_{t-1} = 0.$$

Where $\mathbf{I}_t'$ is the vector of consumer inventories under the counterfactual that consumer k (and

only consumer k) cannot visit a retailer in period t. Note that because each shopper has measure

zero, future prices are independent of shopper k's behavior in period t. Regardless of whether I_{t-1}

is zero or positive, $\delta E(V(\mathbf{I}_t', \mathbf{P}_{t+1} | \mathbf{I}_{t-1}, \mathbf{P}_t))$ is independent of which retailer the shopper visits in

period t, so that maximizing V at time t is equivalent to choosing a retailer to maximize Ψ_{jt}. Ψ_{jt}
can be interpreted as the gain in expected utility associated with purchasing the bundle ($q_{P,t}$, I_t-I_{t-1}
$+q_{S,t}$) from retailer j at prices ($P_{P,t}^j$, $P_{S,t}^j$) relative to the utility received from not visiting any

retailer and simply drawing down the storable inventory by one unit. Because Ψ_{jt} has a straight-
forward interpretation, and facilitates the presentation of retailer choice, we focus on it. When
the shopper has an inventory of $I_t \geq 1$ (and hence chooses $q_{S,t} = 1$) and faces prices

---

[20]   Hereafter, $m_{P,t}$ and $m_{S,t}$ refer to a consumer's purchases at retailer j at
prices $P_{S,t}^j$ and $P_{P,t}^j$.

$P_{S,t}^j$ and $P_{P,t}^j$, we can write Ψ_{jt} as [21]

$$(B.2)\Psi_{jt} = [\beta q_{P,t} + s_L q_{S,t} - P_{P,t}^j q_{P,t} - P_{S,t}^j (I_t - I_{t-1} + q_{S,t}) + \delta E(V(\mathbf{I}_t, \mathbf{P}_{t+1} | \mathbf{I}_{t-1}, \mathbf{P}_t))]$$
$$-s_L q_{S,t} - \delta E(V(\mathbf{I}_t', \mathbf{P}_{t+1} | \mathbf{I}_{t-1}, \mathbf{P}_t)$$
$$=[\beta q_{P,t} + s_L - P_{P,t}^j q_{P,t} - P_{S,t}^j (I_t - I_{t-1} + 1) + \delta E(V(\mathbf{I}_t, \mathbf{P}_{t+1} | \mathbf{I}_{t-1}, \mathbf{P}_t))]$$
$$-s_L - \delta E(V(\mathbf{I}_t', \mathbf{P}_{t+1} | \mathbf{I}_{t-1}, \mathbf{P}_t))$$

Equation (B.2) implies that if retailer j sets $P_{S,t}^j > s_L$ and $P_{P,t}^j < \beta$ then $\Psi_{jt} = \beta - P_{P,t}^j$, since

$\mathbf{I_{t-1}} = \mathbf{I'_{t-1}}$. The relationship between Ψ_{jt} and $P_{S,t}^j$ when $P_{S,t}^J < s_L$ is complicated by the

intertemporal nature of the maximization in equation (B.1). In particular, in the general case

there is no closed-form characterization of Ψ. However, we can obtain a closed-form

expression for Ψ_{jt} when consumer k has inventory I_{t-1}, observes $P_{S,t}^j < \delta^{M+1-I_{t-1}} s_L$, and knows

that storable prices will be s_L or higher for the next M - I_{t-1} periods . Under these conditions, and
assuming $\quad P_{P,t}^j \le \beta \quad$, [22]

_____

[21]   The expression is similar when $I_{t-1} = 0$. There is one potential change in the first
term (the utility from shopping at retailer j) because $q_{S,t}$ may be zero when $I_{t-1}=0$ (i.e., the
consumer may not consume a unit of the storable at time t). There are two changes in the second
term (the counterfactual): the consumer does not consume the storeable in period t (i.e., s_L does
not appear in the second term), and $I_t = I_{t-1}$, rather than I_{t-1} -1.

[22]   Since retailers make zero sales of the perishable if $P_{P,t}^j > \beta$ this condition is
always satisfied in equilibrium.

$$\Psi_{jt} = \left[\begin{array}{l} s_L D_t + \beta - P_{P,t}^j - P_{S,t}^j m_{S,t} + \displaystyle\sum_{\tau=1}^{m_{S,t}+I_{t-1}-1} \delta^\tau (s_L + E(\beta - \min_i(P_{P,\tau+t}^i))) + \displaystyle\sum_{\tau=m_{S,t}+I_{t-1}}^{M} \delta^\tau E(\beta - \min_i(P_{P,\tau+t}^i)) \\ + \delta^{M+1} E(V(\mathbf{I}_{M+t}, \mathbf{P}_{M+t+1} \mid \mathbf{I}_{t-1}, \mathbf{P}_t)) \end{array} \right]$$

$$- \left[s_L D'_t + \sum_{\tau=1}^{I_{t-1}-1} \delta^\tau (s_L + E(\beta - \min_i(P_{P,\tau+t}^i))) + \sum_{\tau=I_{t-1}}^{M} \delta^\tau E(\beta - \min_i(P_{P,\tau+t}^i)) + \delta^{M+1} E(V(\mathbf{I}'_{M+t}, \mathbf{P}_{M+t+1} \mid \mathbf{I}_{t-1}, \mathbf{P}_t)) \right]$$

$$= \sum_{\tau=I_{t-1}}^{I_{t-1}+m_{S,t}-1} \delta^\tau s_L - m_{S,t} P_{S,t}^j + (\beta - P_{P,t}^j)$$

where D_t is a indicator variable that equals 1 if either $I_{t-1} > 0$ or $m_{S,t}^j > 0$ (since in either case, $q_{S,t}$ = 1), and 0 otherwise, and D'_t is a indicator variable that equals 1 if $I_{t-1} > 0$, and 0 otherwise. The first term in square brackets is shoppers k's utility from shopping at retailer j (H_{jt}), and the second bracketed term is her utility if she cannot visit any retailer in period t (H_{0t}).

This expression is maximized at $m_{S,t}^j = M + 1 - I_{t-1}$. To see this, note that if the shopper were to buy $M - I_{t-1}$ or fewer units in period t, she would obtain 0 surplus from the storable for one or more of the next $M+1 - I_{t-1}$ periods, rather than $\delta^\tau s_L$ - $\min_j(P_{S,t}^j)$ in each period.

www.ingramcontent.com/pod-product-compliance
Lightning Source LLC
Chambersburg PA
CBHW081240170526
45165CB00009B/3132